A Kid's Guide to Drawing America™

How to Draw
Colorado's
Sights and Symbols

Jennifer Quasha

The Rosen Publishing Group's
PowerKids Press™
New York

For Dan, Robin, Blake, Jessica, and Wyeth Catlin

Published in 2002 by The Rosen Publishing Group, Inc.
29 East 21st Street, New York, NY 10010

First Edition

Book and Layout Design: Kim Sonsky
Project Editor: Jannell Khu

Illustration Credits: Jamie Grecco
Photo Credits: pp. 7, 20, 22, 24 © Index Stock; p. 8 (photo and sketch) Gift to Rutgers University by Mrs. George F. Ross;
p. 9 (painting) from the collections of the Brooklyn Museum of Art; pp. 12, 14 © One Mile Up, Incorporated; p. 16
© Galen Rowell/CORBIS; p. 18 © Animals Animals; p. 26 © Laura Sivell; Papilio/CORBIS; p. 28 © Richard T. Nowitz/CORBIS.

Quasha, Jennifer
        How to draw Colorado's sights and symbols / Jennifer Quasha
            p. cm. — (A kid's guide to drawing America)
        Includes index.
        Summary: This book describes how to draw some of Colorado's sights and symbols, including the state's seal, the state's
flag, Mesa Verde National Park, and others.
        ISBN 0-8239-6060-9
        1. Emblems, State—Colorado—Juvenile literature 2. Colorado in art—Juvenile literature
  3. Drawing—Technique—Juvenile literature [1. Emblems, State—Colorado 2. Colorado 3. Drawing—Technique]
        I. Title II. Series
        2001
        743'.8'09788—dc21

Manufactured in the United States of America

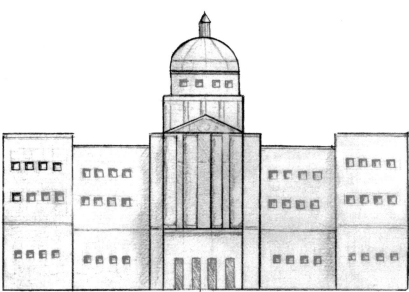

CONTENTS

Let's Draw Colorado

The state of Colorado attracts people year-round. Its Rocky Mountains offer beautiful scenery of snow-capped peaks, even in the summer. There are many sports to enjoy, such as snowboarding, climbing, hiking, and biking. It is a perfect state to visit or live in if you enjoy nature and the outdoors. Colorado has the highest average elevation in the United States. It even has the tallest sand dunes in North America. The Great Sand Dunes National Park, at the foot of another Colorado mountain range, the Sangre de Cristo Mountains, has sand dunes measuring 700 feet (213 m) tall!

Colorado's biggest industries include real estate, tourism, government, health services, transportation, nondurable goods, and communications. Corn, wheat, and hay are major crops grown in Colorado. Cattle meat and dairy products are also a part of the state's agriculture. The state's wealth of natural resources and its mountains can be seen in many of the state's official symbols. You can learn more about these symbols and how to draw them, too. Here are a few hints and tips to help you use this book. All of the drawings begin with a simple shape, and other shapes are added to the first shape. Directions under every drawing explain how to do each step. Each new step is shown in red. The drawing terms below show some of the shapes and words used in this book. The more you practice drawing Colorado's great sights and symbols, the better you will become at drawing. To begin, find a quiet, clean, and well-lit space where you can draw. Good luck and have fun!

The supplies you will need to draw Colorado's sights and symbols are:

- A sketch pad
- An eraser
- A number 2 pencil
- A pencil sharpener

These are some of the shapes and drawing terms you need to know to draw Colorado's sights and symbols:

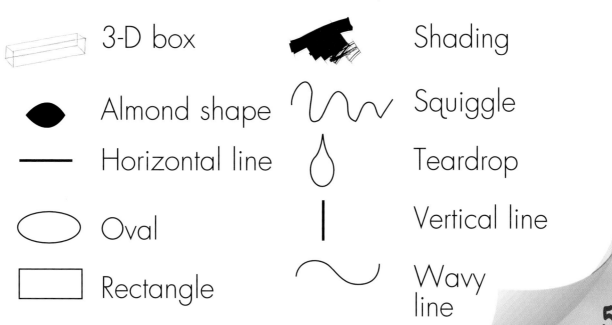

3-D box

Shading

Almond shape

Squiggle

Horizontal line

Teardrop

Oval

Vertical line

Rectangle

Wavy line

The Centennial State

On August 1, 1876, Colorado became the thirty-eighth state to join the Union. Colorado's nickname is the Centennial State because it gained statehood 100 years after America gained its independence. The name *Colorado* comes from a 400-year-old Spanish word that describes the color of the Colorado River. It means "colored" or "the color red." The Colorado River runs through Colorado, and it is from the river's reddish color that the state of Colorado got its name.

Colorado's elevation averages 6,800 feet (2,073 m) above sea level. The highest point in Colorado is Mount Elbert, which is 14,433 feet (4,399 m) tall. Colorado has 104,100 square miles (269,618 sq km) of land and a population of more than four million people. Denver is the capital and the city with the largest population, 497,800 people.

The camper in this photograph has pitched a tent along the Colorado River.

Artist in Colorado

Albert Bierstadt

Some of America's artists were born in other countries. Albert Bierstadt was born in Germany in 1830. He moved to America with his parents in 1832, and he lived in New Bedford, Massachusetts. In 1853, Albert was in his early twenties when he returned to Germany to study art and to travel in Europe. He returned to New Bedford in 1857.

A year later, Albert traveled to the American West. After all of his travels through Europe, he was interested in painting the vast landscapes of Colorado and Wyoming. His many paintings included this landscape painting, *A Storm in the Rocky*

This drawing from Bierstadt's sketchbook was created in pencil and measures 7" x 4½" (17.78 cm x 11.43 cm).

Mountains—Mt. Rosalie. Bierstadt received his first taste of fame when his paintings became sought after by art collectors. He made two more long trips to the West in 1863 and 1871 to enjoy and to sketch the natural beauty of the land. Bierstadt had a great respect for the environment that he visited there. His painting *A Storm in the Rocky Mountains—Mt. Rosalie* captures one of Colorado's many beautiful features, the Rocky Mountains. Although Albert Bierstadt died in 1902, his paintings live on as some of America's greatest landscape art.

Bierstadt's painting *A Storm in the Rocky Mountains—Mt. Rosalie,* painted in 1866, is in the collection of the Brooklyn Museum of Art in New York. It is an oil on canvas, 83" x 142 ¼" (210.8 cm x 361.3 cm).

Map of Colorado

Map of the Continental United States

Colorado borders seven states: Arizona, Utah, Wyoming, Nebraska, Kansas, Oklahoma, and New Mexico. The southwestern corner of Colorado is one quarter of the Four Corners. The Four Corners is the only place in the United States where the borders of four states meet. Although Colorado may be known for its mountains, eastern Colorado is an area of plains and plateaus where wheat, corn, and hay are grown. Colorado has more than ten national forests, including Pike, White River, Uncompahgre, Gunnison, and Rio Grande. The state also has national parks, including Mesa Verde National Park, the site of ancient Anasazi dwellings. The Anasazi were Native Americans who lived 2,000 years ago.

1

To draw map items, start by drawing a slanted rectangle for the outline of Colorado.

2

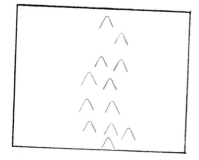

Add upside-down V's to stand for the Rocky Mountains.

3

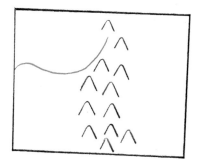

Draw a long, wavy line for the Colorado River.

4

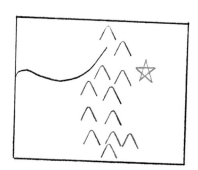

Draw a star to mark the city of Denver, Colorado's capital.

5

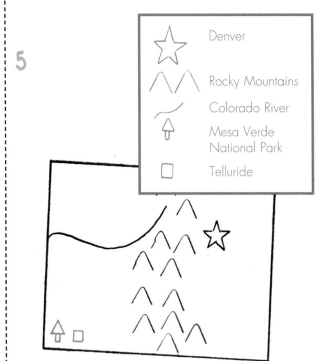

☆	Denver
∧∧∧	Rocky Mountains
⌒	Colorado River
🌲	Mesa Verde National Park
▢	Telluride

a. Draw a square to note the town of Telluride.
b. Draw a tree to show the Mesa Verde National Park.

The State Seal

The Colorado state seal was adopted on March 15, 1877. The seal features a shield divided into two sections. The top half shows the Rocky Mountains. The bottom half shows the tools used by Colorado miners. A white banner under the shield reads *Nil Sine Numine*, which means "Nothing Without the Diety." Deity is another word for God. A triangle above the shield shows the Eye of God with sun rays. The shield has a bundle of sticks and an ax, which stand for strength, authority, and leadership. A slogan, "Union and Constitution," the words "State of Colorado," the year "1876," and six blue stars are on a red band.

1

Start by drawing a large oval.

2

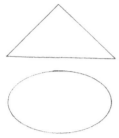

Next add a large triangle above the oval.

3

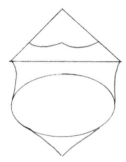

Using the triangle and the oval as a guide, draw the shape of the seal as shown.

4

Draw a straight line across the center of the seal and sketch an outline around the seal. Erase extra lines.

5

Draw two rectangles for the heads of tools.

6

Using the rectangles as guides, draw the shape of the tools and add a large *X* to form the handles.

7

Draw three triangles for mountains in the top half of the seal.

8

Erase extra lines and add details like mountain shapes with snowcaps and clouds. Your seal is done.

The State Flag

The Colorado flag was designed by Andrew Carlisle Johnson. It was adopted on June 5, 1911. The Colorado flag is divided horizontally into three equal-size stripes. The top and bottom stripes are blue and the middle stripe is white. Slightly to the left of the middle of the flag is a red letter C, for Colorado. The C has a golden-yellow ball in its center. This golden ball refers to the gold and other valuable minerals found and mined in Colorado's Rocky Mountains. The red and blue colors of the flag are colors from the American flag. The state flag flies in front of all the official state buildings in Colorado.

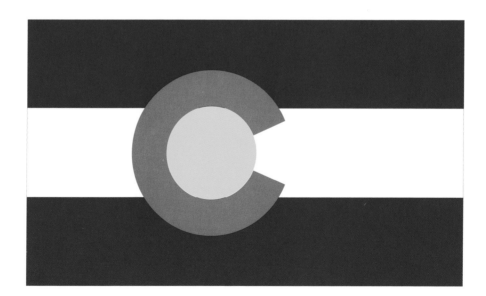

1

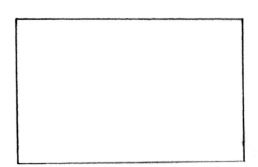

Start by drawing a large rectangle to make the flag's field, or background.

2

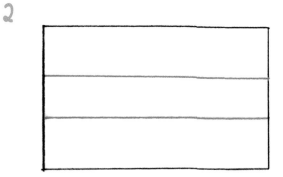

Draw two lines inside the rectangle, dividing the flag into three equal parts.

3

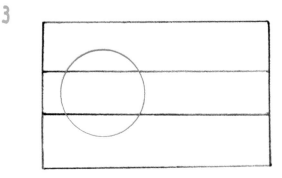

Draw a large circle on the left half of the field.

4

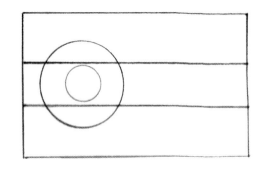

Next draw a smaller circle in the center of the large circle.

5

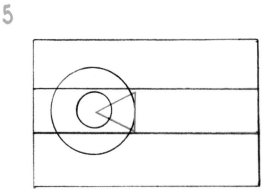

Draw a triangle in the right side of the small circle that starts from the center of the circle and opens out.

6

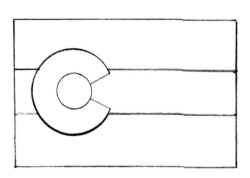

Erase your extra lines and your Colorado flag is complete.

The Rocky Mountain Columbine

The Rocky Mountain columbine was discovered by Edwin Jones on July 10, 1820. He led the first party to climb Pikes Peak, one of Colorado's most famous mountains, that year. Colorado adopted the columbine as the state flower on April 4, 1899. The columbine is

a white and lavender flower. It has five white petals in the center of five lavender petals. It has a yellow center and green leaves. The columbine is a beautiful but fragile flower. In 1925, Colorado passed a law that made it illegal to damage the rare, delicate flower. Today people are allowed to pick no more than 25 columbine flowers or they will be fined a sum of money. The title of Colorado's state song is "Where the Columbine Grows."

1

Draw a small circle in the center of a sheet of paper.

2

Add five narrow rectangles around the circle.

3

Using the rectangles as guides, draw the shapes of the flower's petals. Add five triangles to the flower.

4

Draw the shapes of the flower's purple petals.

5

Add a long, thin line to make the flower's stem.

6

Erase your extra lines. Draw short, wavy lines that fill in the center of the flower.

7

Add detail and shading to finish your flower.

17

The Lark Bunting

Colorado's state bird is the lark bunting. It became the state's official bird on April 29, 1931. The lark bunting does not live in Colorado year-round. Every April flocks of the birds fly into Colorado from the south. Coloradans can spot lark buntings from April to September. They can be seen all over the state, from Colorado's plains to its mountain slopes, which are as high as 8,000 feet (2,438 m). In warm months, male buntings are black with white patches on their wings and tail feathers. The males are about 6 to 7 inches (15–18 cm) long. Female buntings are slightly smaller and are gray-brown with white streaks. In the winter, male buntings turn the same color as the females.

1

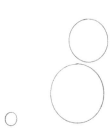

Draw two circles, the smaller, top circle above the bottom circle. Then draw a tiny circle.

2

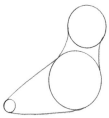

Use long lines to connect your circles to form the bird's body.

3

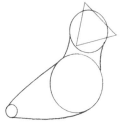

Add a triangle to the bird's head. Make sure you have one point to form the bird's beak and another point for head feathers.

4

Add a long triangle for the tail.

5

Use two triangles and thin, straight lines to draw the bird's legs and feet.

6

Add a long triangle to make the outline of the bird's wing.

7

Make a dot for the bird's eye. Add feathers to wing and head. Erase extra lines and smudges.

8

Add shading and detail. Great job!

The Blue Spruce

The Colorado blue spruce became the state tree on March 17, 1939. The Colorado blue spruce was named by a botanist named C. C. Parry after he discovered it growing on Pikes Peak, in 1862. The blue spruce is a tall, full tree with silvery blue needles. This tree grows in groves of blue spruces, or it can be found mixed in among other trees, such as the ponderosa pine tree, Douglas fir tree, alpine fir, and Engleman spruce. These are some other trees found in the mountain states. The Colorado blue spruce can grow in altitudes from 6,000 to 9,000 feet (1,829–2,743 m) above sea level. In 1892, Colorado schoolchildren voted to have the Colorado blue spruce named the state tree. They had to wait 47 years before their tree earned its official title!

1

Start by drawing a long, thin triangle for the tree trunk.

2

To draw the shape of the tree, add a larger triangle over the thin triangle.

3

Draw branches by adding curvy lines from the tree trunk to the edge of the larger triangle.

4

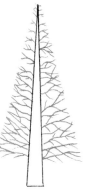

Once you've finished your larger branches, erase the large triangle.

5

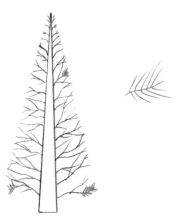

Draw short, straight lines on each branch to create the tree's needles. If you need help, look at the close-up of the needles.

6

Shade in the tree trunk, and the spruce is complete.

The Rocky Mountains

In Colorado, the Rocky Mountain Range covers about 60,000 square miles (155,399 sq km) of land. Also called The Rockies, this famous mountain range has more than 50 peaks that are higher than 14,000 feet (4,267 m). The Rocky Mountain National Park, in Estes, Colorado, is a great place for camping, hiking, fishing, and other fun activities. Its Trail Ridge Road, which crosses the park from east to west, offers magnificent views of the Rocky Mountains' natural beauty. Many animals live in this national park, including owls, elk, bobcats, bears, and Rocky Mountain bighorn sheep. The Rocky Mountain bighorn sheep is also Colorado's official state animal.

1

Begin a mountain range by drawing four uneven triangles. Draw the smallest in the rear to show distance, and the largest in the front.

2

Using your triangles as a guide, draw a soft line that connects the triangles and makes the shape of the mountains.

3

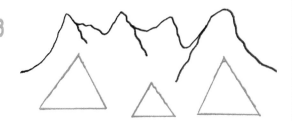

Erase the large triangles and draw three smaller triangles below them to show lower peaks. This helps to show different levels of mountains.

4

Once you've drawn a mountain shape over your smaller triangles, erase extra lines and draw a long line for the ground level.

5

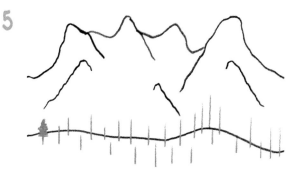

Draw short, straight lines for the trunks of trees. Using the side of your pencil, fill in the leaves on the trees by shading in the shape of a triangle.

6

Add as many trees as you like to make a forest. Once you've finished all of your trees, shade in the mountains and you're done.

Mesa Verde National Park

Mesa Verde National Park, near Cortez and Mancos, Colorado, is a 52,073-acre (21,073-ha) national park that was established in 1906. Mesa Verde means "green table" in Spanish. A mesa is a high, flat area of land that looks like a table. The park contains more than 4,000 sights and 600 cliff dwellings, dating from A.D. 400 to A.D. 1300.

Cliff dwellings are stone houses built into the faces of cliffs and the openings of sandstone caves. Entire villages were built this way. The Mesa Verde cliff dwellings were built by the Anasazi, an ancient people who are believed to be the ancestors of the Pueblo Indians.

1

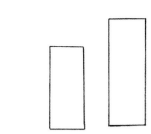

Start by drawing two large, vertical rectangles, noting their placement.

2

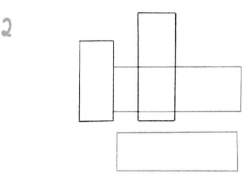

Add two long, horizontal rectangles.

3

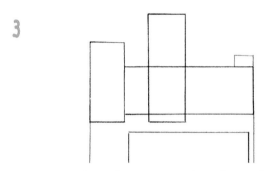

Draw two long lines extending from the right and left sides of your rectangles to form the outline of the cliff dwelling. Add a tiny rectangle on the right side of the top horizontal rectangle.

4

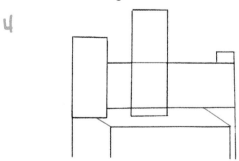

Add two slanted lines to the bottom rectangle to create depth.

5

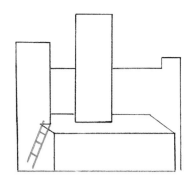

Erase extra lines and smudges. Draw a small ladder at the lower left side.

6

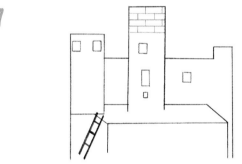

Add squares and rectangles for windows.

7

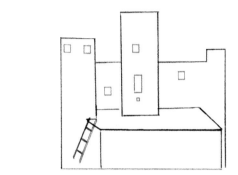

Draw tiny rectangles to make stones and bricks. Fill in the building.

8

Now smudge your drawing a bit to create a ruined look. Add shading and detail. You've created an Anasazi cliff dwelling.

The Colorado Hairstreak Butterfly

Colorado was the thirty-seventh state to adopt a state insect. The Colorado hairstreak butterfly became the state's official insect on April 17, 1996. It begins its life as a caterpillar, and, after a winter of growth, it comes out of its cocoon, which is usually found on the leaf of an oak tree. The hairstreak butterfly has purple wings with spots of orange on their tips and a black border around their edges. The undersides of the butterfly's wings are blue. The wingspan of this butterfly ranges from 1.25 to 1.5 inches (3.2–3.8 cm). It lives in altitudes from 6,500 to 7,500 feet (1,981–2,286 m), and it eats tree sap, aphid honeydew, and raindrops.

1

Start your butterfly by drawing three circles for its head and body.

2

Connect two of the circles to form the butterfly's body.

3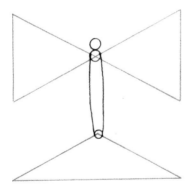

Add three triangles to begin to form the wings.

4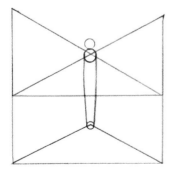

Add three lines to make a rectangle around the bottom triangle.

5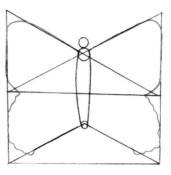

Using your lines as guides, draw the shape of the butterfly's wings.

6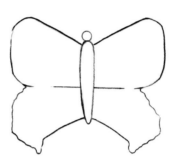

Erase extra lines and smudges.

7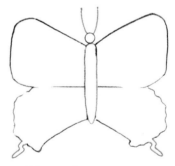

Add two small lines for the butterfly's antennae. Add small, wavy lines at the bottom of the butterfly's wings.

8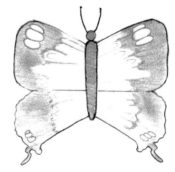

Add detail and shading to finish your butterfly.

Colorado's Capitol

The Colorado state capitol building was designed by E. E. Myers in 1886. The first stone, the cornerstone, was laid on July 4, 1890. It took seven mules to haul this 20-ton (18-t) stone into place. The style of the building is Greek Corinthian. Almost all of the materials used in building came from Colorado, including 240,000 cubic feet (6,796 m^3) of granite and almost 5.5 million bricks. There are 122 cast-iron columns weighing 1.7 tons (1.5 t) each. The gold dome is decorated with 200 ounces (5,670 g) of gold leaf. Although government workers moved in as early as November 1894, the building was not completed until 1908.

1

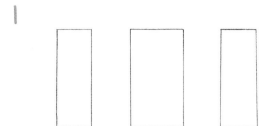

To draw the capitol, draw three large rectangles of equal height. The center rectangle should be a little wider.

2

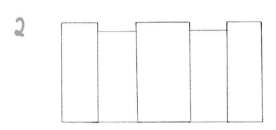

Draw four lines to connect these rectangles and make two new, shorter rectangles.

3

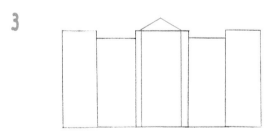

Draw the front entrance of the building by adding a triangle and two thinner rectangles to the center rectangle.

4

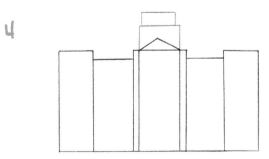

Add two small rectangles over the center to form the base of the dome.

5

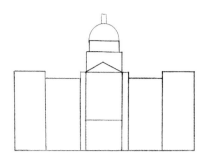

To form the dome, add a line across the center rectangle and a half-circle with a small square above it.

6

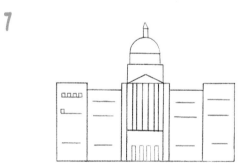

Draw a tiny triangle at the top of your dome. Add six long lines for the columns.

7

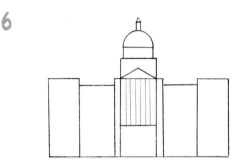

Erase extra lines and smudges. Add squares for windows and rectangles for doors.

8

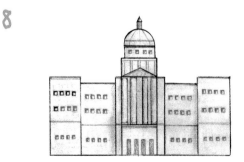

Draw more rectangles to make smaller columns. Add shading and detail to finish the building.

29

Colorado State Facts

Statehood	August 1, 1876, 38th state
Area	104,100 sq m (269,618 sq km)
Population	4,056,100
Capital	Denver, population, 497,800
Most Populated City	Denver
Industries	State and local government, communications, transportation
Agriculture	Cattle, corn, wheat, hay, dairy products
Motto	Nothing Without the Deity
Animal	Bighorn sheep
Folk Dance	Square dance
Fossil	Stegosaurus
Gemstone	Aquamarine
Grass	Blue gamma grass
Song	"Where the Columbine Grows"
Bird	Lark bunting
Tree	Colorado blue spruce
Insect	Colorado hairstreak butterfly
Fish	Greenback cutthroat trout
Flower	Rocky Mountain columbine
Nickname	Centennial State, Colorful State

Glossary

adopted (uh-DAHPT-ed) To have accepted or approved something.

altitudes (AL-tih-toodz) The various heights of objects.

ancestors (AN-ses-turz) Relatives who lived long ago.

ancient (AYN-chent) Very old; from a long time ago.

aphid honeydew (A-fid HUH-nee-doo) A sweet nectar produced in the body of an aphid, a sap-sucking, soft-bodied insect.

archaeological (ahr-key-uh-LAH-jih-kul) Having to do with the study of the way humans lived a long time ago.

botanist (BAH-tun-est) A person who studies flowers.

bundle (BUN-duhl) A group of something.

Corinthian (ko-RIN-thee-un) A type of Greek building design that features highly detailed columns.

cornerstone (KOR-nur STOHN) The first, usually large, stone placed when building a building.

deity (DEE-uh-tee) A god or goddess.

elevation (eh-leh-VAY-shun) The height of an object.

environment (en-VY-urn-ment) All the living things and conditions that make up a place.

granite (GRA-niht) Melted rock that cooled and hardened beneath Earth's surface.

groves (GROHVZ) A group of trees.

horizontally (hor-ih-ZAHN-tih-lee) Sideways.

landscapes (LAND-skayps) Views of scenery on land.

plateaus (pla-TOHZ) Flat areas of land.

resources (REE-sors-ez) Supplies or sources of energy or useful materials.

sand dune (SAND DOON) A mound or ridge of sand that has been piled up by the wind.

sandstone (SAND-stohn) Rock formed over time from tightly packed sand.

symbol (SIM-bul) An object or design that stands for something important.

Index

Web Sites

To find out more about Colorado, check out this Web site:
www.state.co.us